THE SPANISH-AMERICAN WAR

BY
ROGER E. HERNÁNDEZ

Marshall Cavendish
Benchmark
New York

Special thanks to Silvia Marina Arrom, Jane's Professor of Latin American Studies at Brandeis University, for her expert reading of this manuscript.

MARSHALL CAVENDISH BENCHMARK
99 WHITE PLAINS ROAD
TARRYTOWN, NEW YORK 10591-5502
www.marshallcavendish.us

All Web sites were available and accurate when this book was sent to press.

LIBRARY OF CONGRESS CATALOGING-IN-PUBLICATION DATA
Hernández, Roger E.
The Spanish-American War / by Roger E. Hernández.
p. cm. — (Hispanic America)
Includes bibliographical references and index.
ISBN 978-0-7614-4174-8
1. Spanish-American War, 1898—Juvenile literature. I. Title.
E715.H49 2010
973.8'9—dc22
2008033769

Photo research by Tracey Engel

Front cover: *Library of Congress, Prints & Photographs Division*: pga 01889
Title page: The Granger Collection, New York
Back cover: Getty Images/Stock Montage
The photographs in this book are used by permission and through the courtesy of:
Alamy: Paul Thompson Images, 12; AEP, 22. *AP/Wide World Photos*, 37, 67, 69. *Corbis*: 4; Mike Kowalski/Illustration Works, 7; Bettmann, 31, 38, 43, 44, 58. *Getty Images*: Hulton Archive, 29, 51, 61; Stock Montage, 56. *The Granger Collection, New York*: 8, 14, 17, 20, 35, 41, 48, 50, 52-53. *Library of Congress, Prints & Photographs Division*: cph 3b08877, 9; cph 3c01602, 26; cph 3b23178, 33. *New York Public Library*: Picture Collection, The Branch Libraries, Astor, Lenox and Tilden Foundations, 55; Photography Collection, Miriam and Ira D. Wallach Division of Art, Prints and Photographs, Astor, Lenox and Tilden Foundations, 64. *North Wind Picture Archives*, 24.

EDITOR: Joy Bean PUBLISHER: Michelle Bisson
ART DIRECTOR: Anahid Hamparian SERIES DESIGNER: Kristen Branch

Printed in Malaysia
1 3 5 6 4 2

Contents

CHAPTER ONE
The War That Made America a World Power 5

CHAPTER TWO
The Ten Years' War 13

CHAPTER THREE
Cuba's War and America's War 23

CHAPTER FOUR
America Intervenes 39

CHAPTER FIVE
War's Aftermath 59

Glossary 74
Further Information 75
Bibliography 76
Index 77

CHAPTER ONE

THE WAR THAT MADE AMERICA A WORLD POWER

THE SPANISH-AMERICAN WAR OF 1898 WAS BRIEF. Only three and a half months passed between President William McKinley's declaration of war on April 25 and the signing of the *armistice* that ended hostilities on August 12. But its roots sink deep into the history of the countries that saw most of the fighting. And its consequences changed the global balance of power in ways that are still with us today.

Opposite: It was the signing of the armistice that brought the Spanish-American War to a halt. Seen here, President McKinley (standing at end of table) watches as Secretary of State William Day signs the official document.

For Spain, losing the war meant the end of what little remained of its empire. In the 1500s, Spain had become the most powerful country in the world. Its kings ruled parts of modern-day Italy, the Netherlands, parts of central Europe, Latin America, the Philippines in Asia. Spain even controlled a large portion of the United States, including California, Texas,

Colorado, Arizona, and New Mexico. It was one of the largest empires that the world had ever seen. In the late 1600s, however, Spain began to lose its European possessions. Then, in the first few decades of the nineteenth century, most of Latin America, from Argentina to Mexico, freed itself of Spanish colonial rule.

By the time of the war against the United States in 1898, the once great Spanish empire had undergone two centuries of decline. It was reduced to little more than Cuba, Puerto Rico, and the Philippines. After losing the war, Spain lost even those last possessions. This made Spaniards finally accept that their nation no longer ranked among the great powers.

Winning the Spanish-American War moved the United States in the opposite direction. Before 1898, it had been respected as a rich and strong country, but one that largely kept to its own region. The United States generally avoided being involved in the affairs of faraway nations. For instance, in 1848 it defeated neighboring Mexico after a two-year war, but did not get very involved in the revolutions that were taking place in Europe around the same time. In the 1860s, Americans fought a civil war of their own. But after its victory in the Spanish-American War, the United States began to be perceived as a rising power capable of challenging the control of the strongest nations during those years—Great Britain, France, and Germany. This was more than just a perception. It was the start of the American nation's run as the world's superpower.

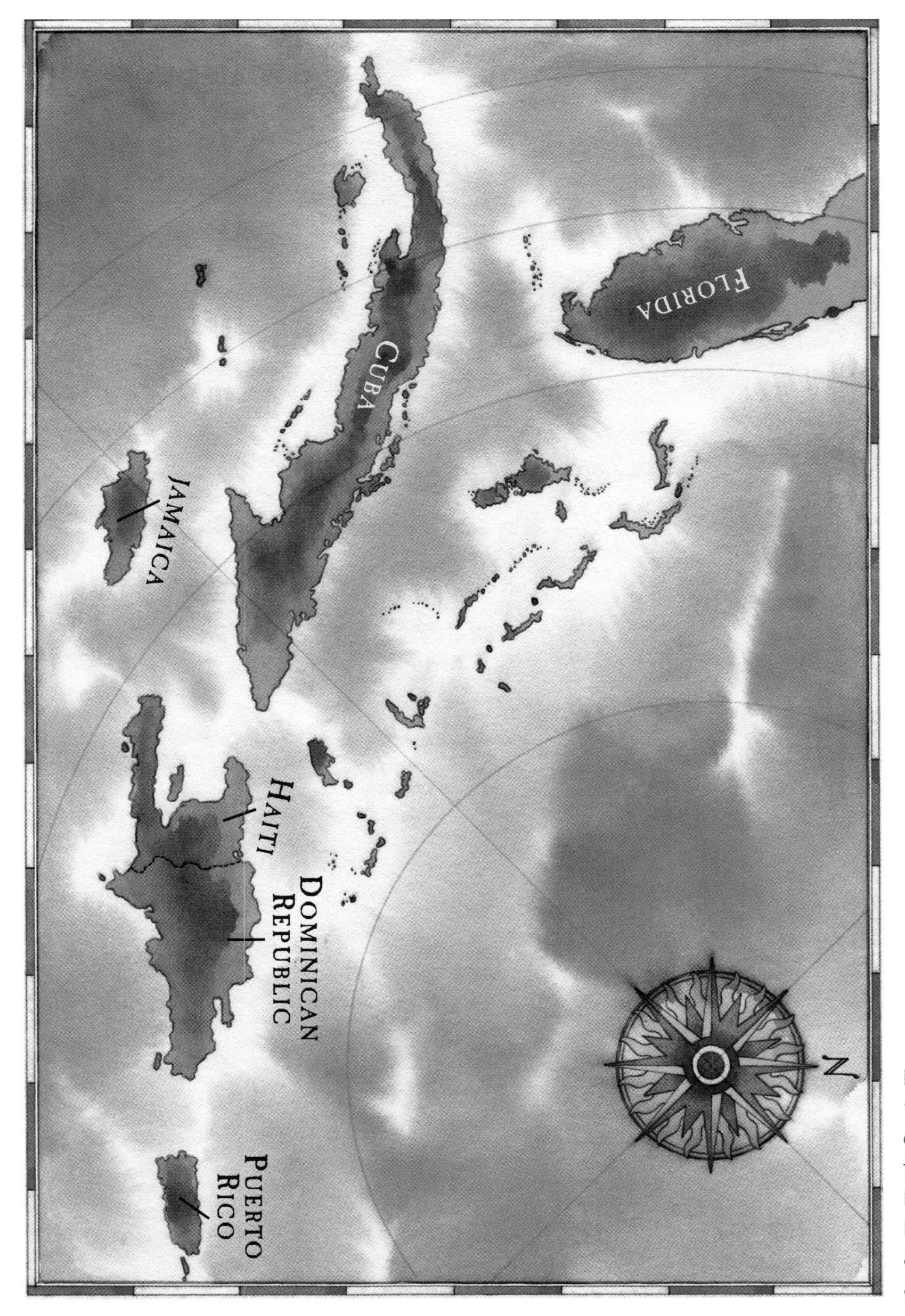

In the late 1800s, Spain still controlled Cuba, the Dominican Republic, and Puerto Rico, among other areas.

A Long Struggle for Independence

In the United States, George Washington became a national hero when he led the war of independence against Great Britain. Similarly, the countries of Latin America have their own national heroes who led wars of independence against Spain.

In Latin America, Venezuela's Simón Bolívar freed the northern part of South America. Argentinean José de San Martin and Chilean Bernardo O'Higgins freed the southern part of the continent. In Mexico, Miguel Hidalgo y Costilla started the struggle that eventually resulted in independence. By the 1820s, the Spanish colonies in the Americas had freed themselves—except Cuba and Puerto Rico.

Simón Bolívar, seen here, was a South American soldier, statesman, and revolutionary leader. He freed the northern part of South America from Spanish rule.

Because they were islands, Cuba and Puerto Rico were isolated from the wars fought in continental Latin America. Also, both islands had large populations of black slaves, which made some of the *criollos*—people of white Spanish descent, born locally—hesitant to seek independence. Criollos in other parts of Latin America had led independence wars against Spain, but in Cuba and Puerto Rico there were wealthy, slave-owning criollos who feared that if Spanish rule ended, slaves would rise up and demand freedom, too.

Nevertheless, criollos disagreed about the situation. Some wanted to end Spanish rule because they thought it was unfair. In the colonial system, only people born in Spain could hold high political office in Cuba or Puerto Rico. Those born locally, even those from the wealthiest upper-class criollo families, were barred from having political power on their own island. It was all a way to keep Cuba and Puerto Rico under the control of Spain. The colonial government did not trust the criollos.

Those who protested the system risked being sent to prison. Even well-off Cubans became resentful. Many of them left for the United States and worked from there to free their country. One of the first people to do this was Félix Varela, a Catholic priest who represented Cuba in the Spanish *legislature*. In 1823, he fled after a controlling government took power in Spain. Varela became an *exile* in New York, where he defended the rights of poverty-stricken Irish who were immigrating in massive numbers at the time. He was also in favor of the independence of Cuba. Varela became a leader of the small Cuban community in the United States. He published some of New York's first Spanish-language newspapers: *El Habanero*

Father Félix Varela was born in Cuba but had to flee the country when he became vocal about fighting for Cuba's independence from Spain.

FÉLIX VARELA

When Father Félix Varela arrived in New York in 1823, immigration from Ireland had just started. Over the decade some 50,000 Irish sailed to America—more immigrants than from any other country. Then, in the 1830s, the number more than tripled to 157,000, according to a 1911 Congressional report.

The Irish were fleeing poverty in Ireland, but when they got to the United States, they encountered prejudice. The Irish were stereotyped as lazy and heavy drinkers. And because they were Catholic, Americans suspected Irish people were more loyal to the pope than they were to the United States. Father Varela, himself a Catholic priest, stood up for these immigrants.

In 1832, Varela founded the School of the Transfiguration of Our Lord in New York. Almost all the students were Irish. That same year there was a *cholera* epidemic in New York. Many doctors refused to go into the Irish neighborhood known as Five Points, where the disease was killing so many people that bodies lay unburied on the sidewalks. Varela set up a temporary hospital in Five Points to tend to the sick. He became a beloved figure in the Irish community.

(*The Havanan*) and *El Mensajero Semanal* (*The Weekly Messenger*). Varela used his publications to demand not only independence for Cuba, but also the abolition of slavery there.

Despite Varela's efforts, Spanish authorities stamped out most pro-independence groups in Cuba and Puerto Rico. One exception was the 1850 plot organized in the United States by the Venezuela-born Narciso López. López, like Varela (who was retired by that time), wanted to liberate Cuba from Spain. Unlike Varela, however, López did not want to abolish slavery. His plan was to keep slavery legal and to make Cuba a state in the Union. He worked with pro-slavery groups of the American South who also wanted Cuba to enter the Union. This would give slaveholding states additional votes in Congress.

From his headquarters in New Orleans and New York, López prepared an invasion on Cuba. In 1850, he and an armed force of some six hundred followers, mostly Americans from southern states, landed in the Cuban city of Cárdenas. They were quickly forced to retreat to Key West, Florida. But even in its failure, the López expedition showed that some Hispanics in the United States were eager to plot the end of Spanish colonial rule in the *Caribbean Sea*.

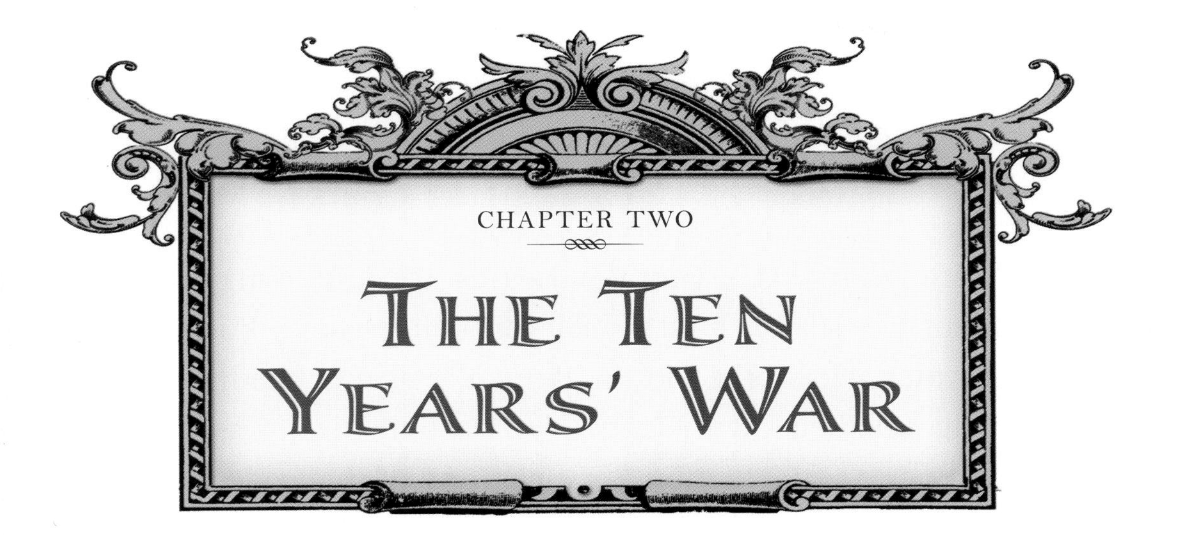

CHAPTER TWO

THE TEN YEARS' WAR

IT WAS NOT UNTIL 1868 THAT CUBAN WARS FOR independence from Spain began in earnest. In October, Carlos Manuel de Céspedes, who owned a sugar mill near the town of Yara, freed his slaves and issued a proclamation calling for an island-wide revolt against Spanish rule. One month earlier, a revolt had also started in the small Puerto Rican town of Lares.

The Lares uprising was crushed almost immediately, and Puerto Rico remained peaceful. But in Cuba, the Yara uprising was the beginning of the Ten Years' War, in which Cuba fought to free itself from Spanish rule. As the fighting raged on in the countryside and the colonial government launched a crack-down against rebel supporters in the cities, Cubans fled their country and sought refuge in the United States. There, like

Opposite: Eugenio María de Hostos was active in striving for Puerto Rican rights. This statue of him stands outside the Santo Domingo library in the Dominican Republic.

others before them, the refugees plotted to help the Cuban independence cause.

The rebels in Cuba appointed a lawyer named José Morales Lemus as their representative in the United States. In Washington, D.C., Morales Lemus tried to convince President Ulysses S. Grant to help his countrymen. Puerto Rican exiles also worked in the United States for the independence of their own island, even though there was no war in Puerto Rico. Ramón Betances, one of the leaders of the failed Lares uprising, spoke out against Spanish rule from his home in New York. Another prominent Puerto Rican activist in New York, Eugenio Maria de Hostos,

Cubans revolt against Spanish rule during the Ten Years' War. Seen here, insurgents stand guard at the coast.

called for the creation of an independent Antillean Confederation made up of Cuba, Puerto Rico, and the Dominican Republic. The confederation was named after the Antilles, which is a name given to the islands in the Caribbean Sea.

The plan never came about. Morales Lemus was unable to convince U.S. authorities to aid the Cuban cause. After many deaths and much destruction, the Ten Years' War ended in 1878 with Spain still in control of Cuba and Puerto Rico.

Plotting from the United States

During the 1880s and into the early 1890s, Cubans and Puerto Ricans in the United States continued to plot to free their islands. Hispanic communities in New York and Key West, Florida, also grew. In 1886, cigar manufacturer Vicente Martinez-Ybor built a third major Cuban American neighborhood—Ybor City, Florida, near what is now downtown Tampa—to house cigar factory workers.

Spaniards settled in Tampa, too, which caused tension between supporters of Cuban independence and those who wanted Cuba to continue being a colony of Spain. It got so tense that Ignacio Haya, a cigar factory owner who sympathized with the colonial government, sought the protection of the Spanish consulate in case he and his family were threatened.

In some ways, however, it was like a family fight. "The

Cubans, while they were bitter in their resentment of Spanish colonial repression, were heavily endowed with Spanish heritage," wrote Frank Trebin Lastra in *Ybor City: The Making of a Landmark Town*.

Through these years, Cubans organized independence clubs in the United States. These social and political organizations kept alive the dream of liberating the island. Every October 10, there were commemorations of the Yara uprising. In his book *City of Intrigue, Nest of Revolution*, Consuelo Stubbins quotes from a man who witnessed Key West's 1890 parade: "A large band of musicians and groups of students . . . marched in the parade, carrying American and Cuban flags. Pictures of Carlos Manuel de Céspedes, Francisco V. Aguilera and Ignacio Agramonte, heroes from previous wars, were displayed at the cemetery."

Sometimes, small groups of armed Cubans sailed from Key West, less than 100 miles (160 kilometers) from Cuba, to try to spark a wider rebellion on the island. Spanish authorities thought these *insurgents* had the silent support of the United States. After one such expedition in 1884, Stubbins said, one Spanish diplomat based in Key West wrote a letter to the foreign ministry in Madrid which said, "The Cubans are supported in these efforts by the local authorities and by the laws of [the United States]. It is impossible for an expedition to enter or leave Key West without being seen by the authorities." In other words, the Spaniards believed Americans were sympathetic to the Cuban cause.

New York City, too, was a hub of Cuban conspiracies. According to Stubbins, the Spanish ambassador called New York "the center for the revolutionary organization" just prior to the start of the War for Cuban Independence in 1895. New York was the place "where plans are made and money is sent in for the rebellion." Many of the preparations were led by José Martí from his office in downtown Manhattan.

José Martí fought fiercely for Cuba's independence. He is seen here as the commander of the Cuban Army.

José Martí

Cubans consider Martí the father of their country. He was born in 1853 and first went to the United States in 1880, after the Spanish colonial government *deported* him from Cuba as punishment for promoting independence. Except for a brief period in Venezuela, Martí lived in New York until he left for the battlefields of Cuba in 1895. While he lived in New York he wrote articles about life in the United States for newspapers in both Venezuela and Buenos Aires. He also wrote poetry. Martí is considered one of the foremost Spanish-language poets of the late 1800s.

JOSÉ MARTÍ: WRITER

José Martí wrote his greatest works while living in the United States and plotting to liberate Cuba. His most famous book, *Versos Sencillos (Simple Verses)* (1891), was written while he was in the Catskills Mountains of New York. Doctors had sent Martí there to rest because of exhaustion brought on by his political activities. The book included a modernized form of Spanish medieval poetry known as the romance.

Martí also covered Cuban and Hispanic issues for the New York newspapers *The Hour* and *The Sun*. In 1889 he also published a magazine for Spanish-speaking children. It was called *La Edad de Oro (The Golden Age)*.

When he was not writing, Martí was plotting to make Cuba independent. Just weeks after he arrived in the United States, he made his first speech in New York's Steck Hall, one of the many meeting halls that dotted New York in the end of the nineteenth century. Martí urged whites, African Americans, and Cubans to fight together for independence. He also tried to unite the aging veterans of the Ten Years' War with younger Cubans like himself, who had less experience but were dedicated to the cause of independence. For the next decade or so in New York, he gave speeches, met with the different pro-independence groups, and began to raise money to fund the war.

Eventually, Martí decided that the growing Cuban communities in Tampa and Key West needed to be included in the struggle for independence. Beginning in the early 1890s, he traveled to Florida and tried to get support from the cigar workers. Some Cubans in Florida did not want an outsider from New York to come in and run their organizations, but Martí persevered and was given roaring welcomes in his first visits.

For instance, upon Martí's arrival in Key West on Christmas Day in 1891, "Thousands of Cubans waving banners of the various clubs greeted him," wrote Stubbins. An eyewitness said, "[Martí] stood up in the carriage, and with his head uncovered, he looked up at the sky and then at the people, who adored him. The crowds were emotionally overwhelmed by his presence."

The following year, Martí founded the Cuban Revolutionary Party, which led to finally uniting most of the pro-independence groups that had been at odds with each other. He spent the next three years traveling between New York and Florida as he organized and raised money. By one count, he visited Tampa at least seventeen times.

Máximo Gómez, a general in the Army during the Ten Years' War, worked with José Martí to fight for Cuban independence.

He also went to Venezuela and the Dominican Republic to speak with Antonio Maceo and Máximo Gómez, two of the foremost veteran generals of the Ten Years' War. Eventually, he convinced them that it was time for another fight for Cuban independence.

Cubans in the United States were getting ready. A *New York Times* story from April 15, 1893, told of some four thousand Cubans taking part in a pro-independence rally in Key West, where "a substantial collection for war expenses was taken." The same story also reported that "a club of seventy-five young men, pledged to Cuban independence," regularly conducted military training in upper Manhattan. "There is a large number of sympathizers with the revolutionary party in New York, and [should the war start] there will be a large influx of fighting men to Cuba."

The Cuban War of Independence

By January 1895, Martí's preparations for war were ready. He had raised enough money to buy three ships and to arm some one thousand fighting men. They were supposed to sail from Fernandina Beach, near Jacksonville, Florida, and land in Cuba to start a revolt. But Spanish colonial officials learned of the plot and alerted U.S. authorities. Martí and the Cubans were in violation of *neutrality laws*, so the federal government stepped in and confiscated the weapons. For Martí it meant a devastating loss of years of work and some $58,000 in ships, supplies, and weapons.

But he continued on with his plans. On February 24 of the same year, an armed uprising in the small town of Baire in Cuba marked the beginning of Cuba's War of Independence. That April, Martí, Máximo Gómez, and a few aides rowed up to the rocky coast of Playitas, in Oriente province. José Martí had finally brought the war to Cuba—but he did not know the fighting he was starting in 1895 would not end until the Americans entered the war against Spain in 1898.

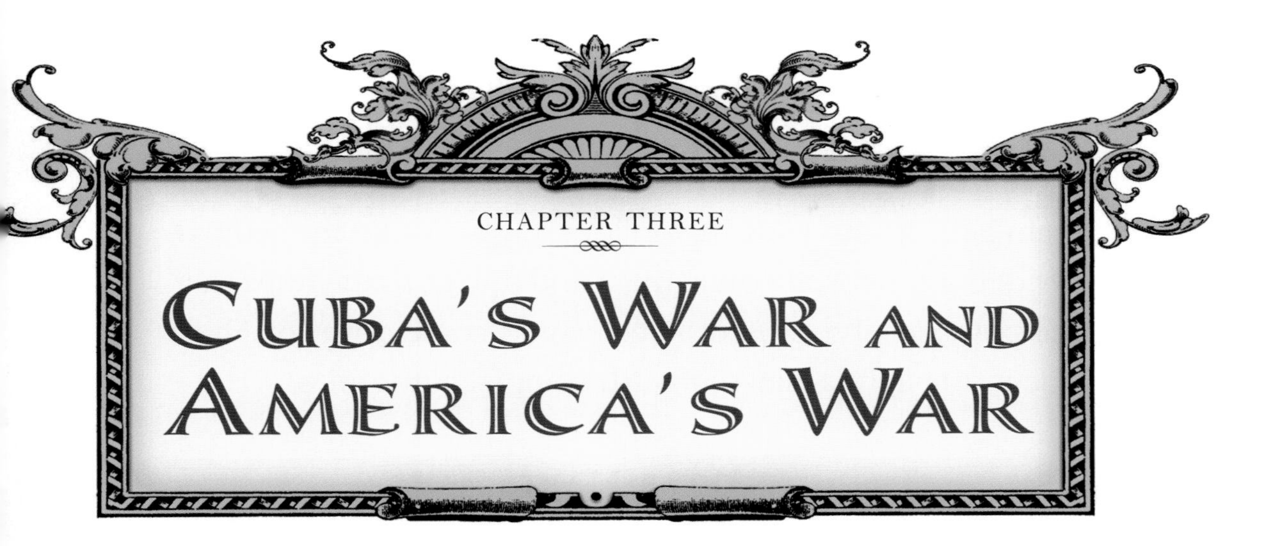

CHAPTER THREE

Cuba's War and America's War

JUST A FEW WEEKS AFTER HE LANDED IN CUBA on April 11, 1895, José Martí was shot to death in a *skirmish* at a village called Dos Rios. Cubans lost the man who for fifteen years had guided their struggle from the United States. He had led the way in uniting rival factions, soothing tensions between black and white Cubans, and convincing some Ten Years' War veterans that there was enough money, manpower, and commitment from the younger generation to start the fight again. Martí remains today the most beloved of Cubans.

Opposite: Cubans still recognize José Martí for all the work he did to free the Cubans from Spanish control. A statue of Martí stands in Havana, Cuba.

Martí was an admirer of American democracy. "One can breathe freely, freedom being here the foundation, the shield, the essence of life," he wrote shortly after he arrived in the United States. But he was also wary of American power. He later wrote that he hoped the independence of Cuba would prevent the United States from controlling Latin America. The men who succeeded Martí as leaders of Cuban Americans were more trusting of Americans' intentions. In fact, one of their main aims in the years that followed was to gain the sympathy of the American government and public, in the hope that the power of the United States would come down on their side in the fight against Spanish colonial authorities.

Tomás Estrada Palma was instrumental in fighting for Cuban independence after José Martí was killed.

After Martí

After Martí's death, two men led Cubans in the United States while the Cuban War of Independence raged on the island: Gonzalo de Quesada and Tomás Estrada Palma. Estrada Palma had been a leader as far back as the Ten Years' War, during which he was imprisoned by the Spanish. After the war he settled in Central Valley, some 30 miles (48 km) north of New York City. He became an American citizen and founded a school for children of well-to-do Hispanic families. He continued to work for Cuban independence, and upon Martí's death Estrada Palma was named chief of the Cuban Revolutionary Party that Martí had founded.

Gonzalo de Quesada was a young leader. He was fifteen years younger than

Martí and thirty-three years younger than Estrada Palma. He was born in Havana, Cuba's capital, in 1868 just two months after the Yara rebellion sparked the Ten Years' War. While he was still a child, his parents moved the family to New York to escape wartime suffering as did many other Cubans. Young Quesada grew up and was educated in the United States. After Martí's death, he became the rebels' chief diplomatic representative in Washington, even though he was only twenty-seven years old.

Having grown up in the United States, Quesada understood Americans' own feelings of patriotism, and he knew how to make persuasive arguments. He and Estrada Palma developed a strategy to gain U.S. sympathy for the cause of independence. They reminded Americans that Cubans' struggle against colonial Spain was like Americans' own struggle against colonial Britain in the Revolutionary War.

"America had her Revolution, her Bunker Hill and Yorktown," Quesada wrote in his book *Cuba's Great Struggle for Freedom*. "The American people are alive to the situation. They recall the gory conflict that made them a free and independent nation." Quesada's book was written in English, aimed directly at the Americans who wanted to know more about the ongoing war between Cubans and colonial Spain.

Independence Activists in the United States

Another way Cubans tried to build support in the United States was by holding Cuban fairs, featuring traditional

Cuban fairs were held in the United States in the late 1800s in order to build support for Cuban independence. This poster was created for the fair to show the men who were the heroes of Cuba at the time.

food, music, and other exhibits about Cuban culture. The purpose was to raise awareness of the Cuban side of the war and to raise funds. "The American people have been so kind to us, and you know we are fighting for the same end as they fought for," one Cuban woman at an 1895 fair told *The New York Times*. The next spring, at Madison Square Garden, Cubans organized what *The New York Times* called "one of the biggest fairs New York has ever seen."

"Pretty Cuban women and their friends will be at the booths, wearing their prettiest gowns. . . . and the home life of Cuba [will be] illustrated several ways," according to an article in *The Times*. Thomas Funston, an American who attended the show, was inspired to go to the island and join the uprising. He later wrote that the fair was supposedly "for the purpose of raising funds for the purchase of hospital supplies for insurgents in the field," but it was likely that the money also went to weapons and military supplies.

There was excitement in Florida's Cuban neighborhoods, too. By 1896, it is reported that Cuban Americans in Tampa had formed forty-one patriotic clubs.

For its part, Key West was, literally, up in arms. Because Florida is located so close to Cuba, it was the ideal jumping off point for Cuban activists to send more fighting men and weapons to the rebels. Fifteen such expeditions landed in

A CAUSE FOR CELEBRATION

The public enthusiasm generated in the United States by the cause of Cuban liberation emerges in a *New York Times* article of May 1, 1898—just one week after the Americans declared war against Spain.

According to the story, 150 young Cuban men "gathered in front of the headquarters of the Cuban Junta, at 56 New Street, and formed into ranks behind the Stars and Stripes and the tricolored flag of Cuba Libre. . . . police held back a crowd of enthusiastic onlookers."

The story makes note of supposed cultural differences by reporting that the Cubans' "greetings were of the emotional character peculiar to the Latin—the embrace taking the place of the American handshake." Nevertheless, the article reports, these Cuban volunteers were Americanized enough to be "armed and equipped by the United States government and sent to Cuba" to fight as American soldiers.

Cuba in 1896. One of the largest brought 750,000 rounds of cartridges, 1,200 rifles, 2,100 machetes, and 400 revolvers, according to a *New York Times* report.

Even in communities without many Cuban residents, Americans were keenly interested in the struggle for independence. "A representative gathering of 1,500 persons met at the opera house this evening to express sympathy for Cuba," says a *New York Times* article about a rally in Wilmington, Delaware. The article goes on to say that a Cuban speaker told the audience that "the Cuban cause was similar to that of the colonists here in 1776," the year of the American Declaration of Independence.

In these gatherings, Puerto Rican independence was not mentioned as often as Cuban independence. Even though Puerto Rican independence activists in the United States worked alongside their Cuban counterparts, back in Puerto Rico there was strong support for *autonomy*. This was an arrangement under which Puerto Rico would remain part of Spain but with enhanced local government and more Puerto Rican participation in the Spanish congress. Some Cubans also supported autonomy for their own island. But the rebels fighting in the battlefields of Cuba and their representatives in the United States made it clear that independence was the only acceptable goal.

"We will not enter into negotiations with the Spanish monarchy [unless it's for] the ultimate independence of the Island of Cuba," Estrada Palma wrote in *The New York Times*.

"All talk of autonomy or reform is a waste of time, as the Cubans will never accept anything else from Spain."

The Fighting in Cuba

While there was peace in Puerto Rico, war raged on in Cuba. Cuba's rebel army, which supporters called the Army of Liberation, fought a *guerrilla*-style campaign, hitting the more powerful Spanish army with quick attack-and-withdraw tactics. The Cubans were only lightly armed. They had little artillery, and not every soldier had a firearm. They relied on cavalry charges in which they carried not the traditional

Members of Cuba's rebel army are seen here at their camp.

sabers of military men on horseback, but machetes, with broad blades used as a tool to cut through vegetation as well as a weapon. In total, there were between 25,000 and 40,000 troops.

The Spanish army, in contrast, relied on the standard military practices of the era—forming infantry squares and standing with rifles and bayonets to fight against cavalry attacks. It was the largest army ever to have crossed the Atlantic Ocean up to that point. In 1897 alone, some 98,000 troops were brought from Spain to fight the Cuban rebels. They joined some 60,000 *voluntarios* (volunteers)—Spaniards who lived in Cuba and wanted to fight the rebels as much as Cubans who opposed independence did.

These voluntarios were highly motivated because they lived in Cuba and wanted to keep it under Spanish control. But the regular army consisted mostly of young men from the countryside of Spain or its urban working class, and they had been *conscripted* against their will. They had little motivation to cross the ocean and fight in the tropical heat for a cause that meant nothing to them. So the Spanish army was weak in spirit, despite its large size and modern weapons.

Two rebel generals, Máximo Gómez and Antonio Maceo, were convinced that one reason for the Cubans' defeat in the Ten Years' War was that the fighting was confined mostly to the eastern third of the island. They resolved to take this war to all of Cuba. Maceo was in charge of leading his 1,600 men westward, out of Oriente

Spanish troops wait to ship out of Santiago Harbor in Cuba during the Spanish-American War.

province, more than 600 miles (966 km) into Havana and beyond to Pinar del Río, on the opposite end of the island.

By early January of 1896, two months after they had started marching, Maceo's troops had fought their way past Spanish army fortifications and had entered the outskirts of Havana. This Invasion of the West—as it has become known in Cuban history—took place in order to cause as much damage as possible to the Spanish army and to the economy overall. Gómez and Maceo believed that the destruction of plantations, sugar mills, and train stations would convince Spain that there was not enough worth fighting for, and Spain would leave Cuba to the Cubans. The Army of Liberation passed like a hurricane, never staying anywhere for long, but leaving death and destruction in its path.

Captain-General Arsenio Martínez Campos, Spain's army chief in Cuba as well as military governor of the colony, realized the dangers of Maceo's troops' presence near the capital city. "A numerous force of separatists is in San José de las Lajas, a city located 29 kilometers [18 miles] from Havana," he wrote. "They have destroyed everything and burned the rail station. . . . families are arriving in Havana from nearby villages, fleeing. The panic is extraordinary."

Martínez Campos resigned from his post and the much harsher Captain-General Valeriano Weyler took over as the army's chief. By February 1896, Weyler had put in motion a strategy of *reconcentration*. His plan was to force those living on farms and in small villages into camps surrounded by barbed wire and guarded by Spanish Army troops. They did this so that the rebels could not have the support of the rural population. These camps had unsanitary conditions and were always short of food, yet people were supposed to stay there as long as the war was being fought. Tens of thousands of Cubans starved to death.

The Spanish Army kept a number of Cubans at a reconcentration camp in order to keep them from fighting for independence for their country.

Militarily, the plan did not work as Weyler hoped. "These extreme measures nevertheless failed to crush the insurrection, because the rebels retreated to rural areas in the eastern provinces and from there carried on guerrilla operations," historian José M. Hernandez wrote in a Library of Congress report. "Since the Spaniards were unable to defeat the rebels and the rebels lacked the resources to drive them from the island, no one knew for certain how long it would continue."

The World Watches

Politically, Weyler's reconcentration policy was a disaster for the Cuban government. Other nations became horrified at the sight of bone-thin Cuban children dying at the camps, and foreign governments blamed Spain. Anger was especially widespread in the United States, where newspapers carried photos of starving families and stories of terrible things done by Spanish troops. In particular, the *New York Journal* and its rival *New York World* tried to outdo each other. Both newspapers were filled with articles showing Cubans as the helpless victims of Spaniards' cruelty. They were using the war in Cuba to get ahead in their battle to see which could sell more newspapers. Some of the stories were untrue or exaggerated, but the coverage encouraged the United States to *intervene*.

Public outrage was strong just weeks after Weyler put his policy into effect. The U.S. Congress abandoned its official *neutrality* and passed a resolution urging the recognition of Cuban independence. President Grover Cleveland, in his last days in office, ignored it. But the incoming president, William McKinley, had campaigned on a platform that included support for Cuban independence. The United States, it seemed, was ready to take sides.

After McKinley was inaugurated in March 1897, he increased pressure on Spain to find a settlement. However, he did not officially recognize the rebels, and he insisted he did not want the United States to go to war. Spain's response was to stand tough. Cuban prime minister Antonio Cánovas del Castillo swore to fight to "the last man and the last penny" to keep Cuba under Spanish control. He said to the Spanish congress, "The conservation of

A campaign poster from 1896 shows William McKinley as the Republican party candidate for president.

the island of Cuba is in the sentiment, is in the heart of all Spaniards."

That summer, Cánovas del Castillo was assassinated by an Italian *anarchist*. The man who became the next prime minister of Cuba was Práxedes Mateo Sagasta. He took a more moderate view of the situation in Cuba. Weyler was let go as chief of the army and Sagasta closed the reconcentration camps, and offered autonomy to Cuba and Puerto Rico.

Autonomist governments, still under Spanish rule but now with the power to make decisions over local matters, took office on both islands early in 1898. The autonomist system was welcome in Puerto Rico, where it had widespread support. Cubans might have embraced it as well, especially because Antonio Maceo had been killed in battle that December, and the rebels were left without their most successful field commander. But the arrangements did not make the the Spanish or the Cubans happy. Cubans in the United States, as well as those fighting in the countryside, continued to demand full independence. Pro-Spain voluntarios rioted in Havana because they thought autonomy weakened Spanish power and betrayed the Spaniards who had died to keep Cuba a colony.

In the midst of the crisis, as sympathy for Cubans grew stronger and calls for intervention grew louder, the United States sent the battleship *U.S.S. Maine* to Havana. The visit was meant to display U.S. power and to protect American citizens in Havana who might be hurt by the rioters. That

February of 1898, an explosion blew up the *Maine*, and 266 sailors were killed. Cubans, as well as Americans who wanted the United States to intervene, blamed Spain for the attack and called for war.

A photo of the *U.S.S. Maine* on February 16, 1898, a day after an explosion sank the battleship in the Havana harbor, killing 266 crew members.

863,956 WORLDS CIRCULATED YESTERDAY

The World.

"Circulation Books Open to All."

NEW YORK, THURSDAY, FEBRUARY 17, 1898.

VOL. XXXVIII. NO. 13,339.

MAINE EXPLOSION CAUSED BY BOMB OR TORPEDO?

Capt. Sigsbee and Consul-General Lee Are in Doubt---The World Has Sent a Special Tug, With Submarine Divers, to Havana to Find Out---Lee Asks for an Immediate Court of Inquiry---Capt. Sigsbee's Suspicions.

CA I. SIGSBEE, IN A SUPPRESSED DESPATCH TO THE STATE DEPARTMENT, SAYS THE ACCIDENT WAS MADE POSSIBLE BY AN ENEM

Dr. E. C. Pendleton, Just Arrived from Havana, Says He Overheard Talk There of a Plot to Blow Up the Ship---Cap Zalinski, the Dynamite Expert, and Other Experts Report to The World that the Wreck Was Not Accidental---Washington Officials Ready for Vigorous Action if Spanish Responsibility Can Be Shown---Divers to Be Sent Down to Make Careful Examinations.

The New York World a day after

who had been Populists and those who became Progressives — clamored for the United States to rescue the Cuban people from the Spanish malefactors.

President William McKinley and the conservative Republican leaders in Congress reluctantly gave way before this pressure. Senator Henry Cabot Lodge warned McKinley, "If the war in Cuba drags on through the summer with nothing done we [the Republican party] shall go down in the greatest defeat ever known."

Already, in November 1897, Spain, at the urging of President McKinley, had granted

CHAPTER FOUR

AMERICA INTERVENES

NOT EVERYBODY WANTED THE UNITED States to declare war on Spain. President McKinley did not want to fight, even though he pressured Spain for a settlement in Cuba. Even Cuban leaders in the United States, who had tried to gain American sympathy for years, were not so sure about going to war.

"We oppose any intervention that does not have for its declared object the independence of the island," Gonzalo de Quesada, the rebels' representative in Washington, told the House of Representatives Committee on Foreign Affairs. Quesada wanted the United States to officially recognize the temporary government that the rebels had set up in the parts of Cuba's countryside that they controlled. Quesada said about a quarter-million Cubans had pledged allegiance to this

Opposite:
A headline in the New York *World* newspaper from February 17, 1898 blames Spain for the explosion without any real evidence. This helped spread pro-war sentiment in the U.S.

rebel republic. From his Washington office, he later issued a statement reporting that the rebel government had its own constitution, legislature, president, and even schools.

A Spanish investigation said that an accidental internal explosion had caused the *Maine* ship to sink. Some historians have even speculated that Cuban rebels blew it up to draw the United States into the war. But U.S. newspapers blamed it on a Spanish attack. The *New York Journal* stepped up the pressure with a headline dedicated to the war in Cuba. The paper called for the United States to enter the war against Spain.

"Why did they blow up our *Maine*?" asked an American sailor named Worth Bagley in a letter to his mother, as quoted in *The War of 1898: The United States and Cuba in History and Historiography* by Louis A. Pérez Jr. "The cause of the war lies in a set of American colors blown up in an explosion, and with the colors the men who served to protect them; blown up at night while asleep—evidence in itself sufficient to show that a contemptible Spaniard did it. The blood almost fills my head when I think of this; it makes me almost wild with anger." Bagley, as it turned out, became the first American military officer killed in the war.

To this day, no one really knows the cause of the explosion. But after it happened, sentiment for war against Spain reached a new high. Congress authorized President McKinley to issue an ultimatum to Spain: leave Cuba, or the United States will use military force to throw you out.

This Joint Resolution of the House of Representatives and the Senate also declared, "The Island of Cuba is and by right ought to be free and independent," which went only halfway in pleasing the rebels. The promise that the United States would not attempt to govern Cuba met the long-standing demand for independence, going back to before the Ten Years' War. But the resolution did not recognize the rebel government—a decision that would have consequences later in the war as well as for future U.S.-Cuba relations.

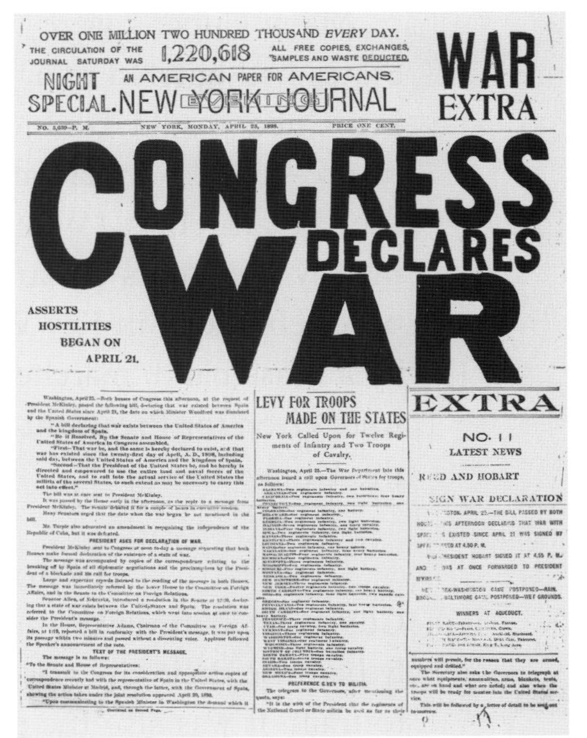

OVER ONE MILLION TWO HUNDRED THOUSAND *EVERY* DAY.
THE CIRCULATION OF THE JOURNAL SATURDAY WAS 1,220,618 ALL FREE COPIES, EXCHANGES, SAMPLES AND WASTE DEDUCTED.
AN AMERICAN PAPER FOR AMERICANS.
NIGHT SPECIAL. NEW YORK JOURNAL
WAR EXTRA
NO. 5,639—P. M. NEW YORK, MONDAY, APRIL 25, 1898. PRICE ONE CENT.

CONGRESS DECLARES WAR

ASSERTS HOSTILITIES BEGAN ON APRIL 21.

Washington, April 25.—Both houses of Congress this afternoon, at the request of President McKinley, passed the following bill, declaring that war existed between Spain and the United States since April 21, the date on which Minister Woodford was dismissed by the Spanish Government:

"A bill declaring that war exists between the United States of America and the kingdom of Spain.

"Be it Resolved, By the Senate and House of Representatives of the United States of America in Congress assembled,

"First—That war be, and the same is hereby declared to exist, and that war has existed since the twenty-first day of April, A. D., 1898, including said day, between the United States of America and the kingdom of Spain.

"Second—That the President of the United States be, and he hereby is directed and empowered to use the entire land and naval forces of the United States, and to call into the actual service of the United States the militia of the several States, to such extent as may be necessary to carry this act into effect."

The bill was at once sent to President McKinley.

PRESIDENT ASKS FOR DECLARATION OF WAR.

TEXT OF THE PRESIDENT'S MESSAGE.

LEVY FOR TROOPS MADE ON THE STATES

New York Called Upon for Twelve Regiments of Infantry and Two Troops of Cavalry.

Washington, April 25.—The War Department late this afternoon issued a call upon Governors of States for troops, as follows:

PREFERENCE GIVEN TO MILITIA.

EXTRA

NO. 11
LATEST NEWS

REED AND HOBART SIGN WAR DECLARATION

WINNERS AT AQUEDUCT.

On April 25, 1898, the front page of the New York Journal announces the declaration of war on Spain.

Spain saw the ultimatum as unacceptable. The Spanish government refused American demands. Diplomatic relations were cut, and on April 25, 1898, the United States formally declared war on Spain. The Cuban rebels were not named as participants in the conflict, even though much of the fighting would take place on Cuban soil, and the United States refused to recognize the rebel government. But Congress passed and the president signed the Teller Amendment, in which the U.S. government pledged "to leave the government and control of the island to its people" after Cuba was stable.

Many Cubans were thrilled that the powerful United States had entered their war against Spain while promising Cuba would be independent at some time in the future—even if Americans did not officially acknowledge the Cuban rebels. "Wherever the eye turns to-night it is met by the colors of Cuba," said a *New York Times* report on celebrations in Key West. "Some 200 Cubans, headed by a brass band, marched through the streets. . . . cheers were given for President McKinley and the newspapers of the United States."

Troops in Tampa

Cubans in Tampa were in a celebratory mood, too, especially because their city was where American troops gathered to train. It was also the place troops would leave from for the invasion of Cuba. Some 25,000 fighting men arrived, but they faced severe backups settling in and getting supplies. Only two rail lines went into Tampa, and only one line led to Tampa Bay. There the transport ships awaited, able to use only the one wharf that had been built. Supplies were delayed. The men arrived in town after long delays, and they had to wait even longer to ship out.

These soldiers, edgy as they waited for battle, sometimes behaved badly. Historian Frank Trebin Lastra tells of a mob of military men that rioted, breaking up a number of Ybor City businesses. Still, many Cubans in Ybor considered it an isolated incident and overall gave the soldiers a warm

On a street in New York City, recruiters try to get young men to volunteer to fight in the Spanish-American War.

reception. The Cubans were happy to see that the powerful U.S. Army was going to help liberate their island from Spain. One story is told about men from the famous cavalry regiment, the Rough Riders, entering Las Novedades Restaurant in Ybor on horseback, after which owner Manuel Menéndez gave the soldiers a round of drinks on the house. "For the Cuban community in Ybor City, the war brought pride, excitement and hope," wrote Lastra.

Meanwhile, some Spaniards in Tampa moved out. They felt threatened by rising hostility from local Cubans excited by the presence of the troops. One of the largest social clubs for Spaniards, the Centro Español, closed its doors. Prominent members of the community met with a pro-Spain cigar factory owner and told him they needed the

This photo shows a number of troops waiting to set sail from Tampa, Florida to Cuba to start fighting the Spanish-American War.

protection of city officials. He met with Fernando Figueredo, the Cuban mayor of the municipality of West Tampa, who said that his " greatest wish was that more cordial relations be established among members of the Spanish-speaking communities."

There was another Spanish-speaking community in the United States, nearly 2,000 miles (3,220 km) away, for whom the war posed a different problem.

Hispanic New Mexicans Suspected of Spanish Sympathies

The Southwest of the United States had been colonized by Spain beginning in 1598, when Juan de Oñate crossed the Rio Grande into what is now New Mexico. That was even before the English established their first colony, in Jamestown, Virginia, in 1607. The region remained under the control of Spain until 1821, when Mexico defeated colonial Spanish forces and became an independent nation. Then, in the Mexican-U.S. war of 1846–1848, the United States won from Mexico the lands that eventually became the American states of Arizona, California, Colorado, New Mexico, and Texas.

In that newly American territory lived Spanish-speaking descendants of the original Spanish settlers who had colonized the region more than two hundred years earlier. But they were few in number and spread widely apart, so English speakers soon started to outnumber Spanish speakers almost everywhere—except in New Mexico. When it became a U.S. territory in 1850, New Mexico was home to 57,000 *Hispanos*, as they have become known, and just 2,000 Anglos (whites). Thirty years later, some 80,000 New Mexicans were Hispanic, and only 10,000 were Anglo.

The American Spanish speakers were proud of their Hispanic culture. That pride brought them under suspicion when the United States and Spain went to war. "As a rule, the Spanish-speaking part of the population has given all

MAKING NEW MEXICO A STATE

In his book *The Language of Blood*, historian John Nieto-Phillips wrote that "rumors began to circulate throughout New Mexico" that "Nuevomexicanos did not want to fight against their mother country, Spain." Americans began to doubt whether New Mexico, classified as a territory since 1850, should become a full-fledged state. Could Hispanos ever be loyal Americans?

The pro-statehood campaign went back to the years before the Civil War. A decade later, the Territorial Legislature voted to ask Congress to grant New Mexico statehood. Two years later, Congress voted down the idea.

Five similar proposals also failed in the years before the Spanish-American War.

In 1912, New Mexico finally became a state.

its sympathy to Spain," reported *The New York Times* in August 1898, "and has demonstrated . . . a deep hostility to American ideas and American policies."

The article claimed that Hispanos were not learning English, but it did not cite any specific evidence of "sympathy" toward Spain or "hostility" to the United States. Still, suspicions were widespread. In his book *Spanish Redemption,* Charles Montgomery wrote that one Anglo New Mexican complained to territorial governor Miguel Antonio Otero that "at least three quarters of the population were Spanish sympathizers." Otero, himself a descendant of the early Spanish settlers, responded that even though "Spanish blood courses through the veins of many an American citizen today, I do not believe that fact should justify an American citizen in upholding the actions of Spain."

Local Spanish-language newspapers also defended Hispanos' patriotism. One poem published in *El Nuevo Mexicano* said, in translation:

> On the battlefield
> like good patriots
> and faithful Americans
> we will free from that yoke
> the humble Cuban

Among those faithful Americans were about a thousand Spanish-surnamed New Mexicans who fought in the Spanish-American War. That total included twelve Hispanos who volunteered for the famed Rough Riders cavalry regiment. Foremost among them was Maximiliano Luna, a member of one of New Mexico's best-known Hispano families. Historian Charles Montgomery wrote in *Spanish Redemption,* "As U.S. troops mobilized in Tampa, [Luna] reportedly demanded an assignment at the front ranks so that he, a 'man of pure Spanish blood,' might

Hispanos were among the soldiers who volunteered for the Rough Riders cavalry regiment.

demonstrate his loyalty to the Union." Luna did go to the front, and he was commended for bravery at the Battle of San Juan Hill.

From Daiquirí to San Juan Hill

One of the first direct contacts between American officers and Cuban rebel officers in the field was the message taken in early May 1898 by U.S. Army lieutenant Andrew S. Rowan to General Calixto García. It was an effort by American commanders to seek the cooperation of García, whose troops controlled interior areas of Oriente province near Santiago de Cuba, where the American war planners were looking to land invading forces. After all the prewar publicity about valiant Cubans waiting for U.S. help, this first contact between rebel fighters and the U.S. Army became well known in the American popular imagination. The "Message to Garcia" was made into two movies, in 1916 and 1936.

On June 20, a U.S. Navy fleet of 42 ships carrying some 16,200 soldiers appeared off the coast of Santiago, Cuba's second-largest city. Before launching the main invasion in Santiago, Admiral William Sampson and General William R. Shafter met with García to plan early attacks outside the city. It was agreed that Cuban and American forces would first take the nearby village of Daiquirí.

As García wrote in his official report of the battle, close to a thousand Cuban troops "advanced on Daiquirí, rapidly displacing the Spanish troops that were there. As the Cubans took Daiquirí, cannons on U.S. ships began to attack the position. However, as soon as the Cuban flag was raised, the U.S. shelling stopped. The U.S. Army landed its first regiments at Daiquirí and advanced on Firmeza and Siboney, led by Cuban troops who were the first to occupy these villages."

U.S. troops arrive at Daiquirí, Cuba on June 22, 1898 to fight in the Spanish-American War.

The Americans and Cubans faced light resistance, because Santiago and the nearby area were not heavily defended. The Spanish army had 24,500 soldiers in Oriente, but instead of mainly being at Santiago, they were spread throughout the province. Historian Kenneth E. Hendrickson, in his book *The Spanish-American War*, wrote that the Spanish commanding general, Arsenio Linares Pomba, "chose not to move any of his forces, fearing that any location he evacuated would be overrun by Cuban insurgents."

As the Cuban and American allies prepared to attack Santiago from their base at Daiquirí, relations between them were friendly at first, but then began to go downhill. "After observing them for a short time, most American fighting men concluded that the Cubans were thieves and liars and almost useless in battle," Hendrickson wrote. But historian Louis Pérez argues that Cubans fought well: "Cubans played a decisive if largely unacknowledged role in the U.S. victory. . . . they engaged in military operations at critical moments of the campaign. Cubans secured the beaches and facilitated the landing of U.S. forces. A division under the command of General Demetrio Castillo Duany secured the designated landing site at Daiquirí."

A group of soldiers in the Spanish-American War stand ready to defend their camp with bayonets at the ready.

Still, the Cubans got little respect from U.S. troops. It was the beginning of a clash of cultures between supposed allies. Before the war, Americans had an idea of Cubans as brave freedom fighters. But once they landed in Cuba, they began to mistrust the Cubans they met, many of whom were of African ancestry and were dressed in rags. In turn, Cubans' desire for American help in their war against Spain became mixed with suspicion that the United States wanted to control Cuban affairs.

General Shafter's main force of 15,000 Americans marched closer toward San Juan, as did 4,000 Cubans under General García. They took the Spanish fort of El Viso and the town of El Caney, in Santiago's outskirts. Next on the road to the city was San Juan Hill, defended by a small unit of 850 Spaniards.

A mostly American force began the assault on July 1. The U.S. troops slowly made their way up the hill under intense Spanish fire. The Spanish soldiers, although few in number, fought fiercely and caused heavy American casualties. But an American artillery attack, followed by a charge led by future president Theodore Roosevelt and his Rough Riders, finally forced the Spaniards to withdraw to defensive lines closer to Santiago.

As it turned out, San Juan Hill was the only major land battle of the war. Santiago itself was still in Spanish hands, as was the rest of the island. In the battle, the Americans suffered more casualties than the Spanish (223 Americans died and 1,243 were injured; the

Opposite: A scene from the battle at San Juan Hill.

Spanish had 102 dead and 552 injured), and tropical illnesses made a lot of soldiers sick. So the Americans were not even sure they had gained a victory. "Tell the President for heaven's sake to send us every regiment and above all every battery possible," Roosevelt wrote to his friend, Senator Henry Cabot Lodge, as written by historian Hugh Thomas in *Cuba: The Pursuit of Freedom*. "We are within measurable distance of a terrible military disaster."

A bloody battle loomed ahead for control of the city of Santiago, which was defended by 12,000 newly reinforced Spanish troops. What if they fought as hard as the 850 who had defended San Juan Hill? The Americans braced for a Spanish counterattack.

Battle for Santiago

A counterattack never came. At San Juan Hill, facing a live-or-die situation, Spanish troops had fought well. But in Santiago, because of a shortage of food and perhaps also because they had more time to think about the cause for which they were fighting, the Spanish soldiers just wanted to go home. Still, the Americans did not know of the Spaniards' weakness, and they prepared for a siege.

Then a tactical mistake by Captain-General Blanco, the Spanish military governor in Havana, literally sank Spain's already slim chances of winning the war. The Spanish fleet anchored at Santiago Bay was ordered to leave the port and try to break the U.S. naval blockade. Admiral Pascual

The naval battle at Santiago is depicted here.

Cervera y Topete, who was in charge of the Spanish ships, knew this strategy was doomed to fail. The "blockading fleet is four times superior to our own; our destruction is absolutely guaranteed if we leave port," he said, according to Thomas.

He was right. U.S. firepower destroyed all the Spanish ships, and 350 sailors died. No American ship suffered serious damage, and just one American sailor was killed.

The naval battle left Santiago unable to supply itself—the U.S. Navy controlled the entrance to the port, and American and Cuban troops controlled the roads into the city. Also, the U.S. could now attack the city not only from artillery positions on land, but also from huge naval guns on battleships, without having to worry about opposition from the Spanish navy. To escape the danger and lack of food, most civilians, Cubans and Spaniards alike, left the city.

The U.S. bombardment began on July 10. It lasted three days and caused little damage to civilian buildings, but knocked out the Spanish artillery. Almost out of food and with troops unwilling to die for the cause of keeping Cuba a colony of Spain, Spanish authorities surrendered Santiago and the entire province of Oriente to U.S. forces on July 17.

On July 17, 1898, General Jose Toral (center right) surrenders at Santiago, Cuba to the American commander, Major General William Shafter (center left).

The War in Puerto Rico

Eight days later, with the war in Cuba practically over, about three thousand soldiers made the first U.S. landing in Puerto Rico—another Spanish colony from which the United States wanted to oust Spain. There had been no uprising there prior to the Americans' arrival as there had been in Cuba, so the invasion went much more smoothly. The troops met little resistance from Spanish troops and much applause from Puerto Ricans, who regarded them as liberators. By July 28, 1898, American troops held the large city of Ponce, where they issued a proclamation saying that the United States had invaded to bring Puerto Rico a "banner of freedom."

Over the first week in August, Americans and Spaniards fought skirmishes near the cities of Coamo and Mayagüez. But these clashes were minor. American losses for the entire Puerto Rico campaign were very small: seven killed and thirty-six wounded.

Then, on the twelfth of that month, all fighting stopped. Spain and the United States signed an armistice ending the war and giving the United States possession of Cuba and Puerto Rico. Neither Cubans nor Puerto Ricans were invited to take part in negotiations.

EVEN BEFORE CUBA AND PUERTO RICO WERE excluded from the armistice talks in August, Cuban anger at their American ally had been simmering. The ethnic mistrust that began among rank-and-file troops spread to the top officers. General Calixto García, in particular, felt deeply insulted that he, as the head of Cuban forces in Oriente province, had been ignored by American commanders during the surrender of Santiago in July.

"I was not honored by a single word from you regarding peace negotiations or the terms of surrender proposed by the Spaniards," he wrote to General Shafter. Citing rumors that the Americans feared Cuban troops would run riot and lynch Spaniards, García added:

> Permit me to protest against the merest shadow of such an idea, because we are not a savage people

Opposite: General Calixto García, the general of the Cuban forces, became angered with American commanders when they did not mention the Cuban efforts during the surrender of Santiago.

> without knowledge of the laws of civilized war. We are a hungry and ragged army, like the army of your ancestors in your own war of independence. But like the heroes of [the U.S. Revolutionary War], we respect our cause too much to stain it with barbarity and cowardice.

García was so livid that he submitted his resignation to General Máximo Gómez, the overall commander of the Cuban army.

García was quickly convinced to take the job back, however. The U.S. government, at least unofficially, said the failure to include García had not been intentional. *The New York Times* quoted one "member of the Cabinet" as saying that if "García was not invited to participate in the ceremonies attending the raising of the American flag over Santiago, it was a mistake." In September, he was finally allowed to enter Santiago "as a U.S. guest."

Cuban civilian authorities also tried to downplay the incident. "We truly appreciate the great and generous conduct of the United States in coming to our aid for the sole purpose of liberating us from the Spanish yoke," said Domingo Capote, vice president of the rebel government in a *New York Times* article from July 1898. "We have the utmost faith in the pledges made in our behalf that we enjoy our liberty as an independent Republic." This was an attempt to repair relations with American officials—while at the same time reminding them that in the Teller Amendment the United States had promised Cuba its independence.

Cuban armies, such as this group of volunteers, fought in the Spanish-American War, yet their efforts were not recognized by the United States.

Under American Rule

The armistice talks in the summer of 1898 ended the fighting and left the United States in possession of the former Spanish colonies of Cuba, Puerto Rico, and the Philippines. What would become of them was yet to be decided as American and Spanish officials sat down in Paris to negotiate the final peace treaty.

In Puerto Rico, there was not a lot of movement for independence. One of the best-known Puerto Rican lead-

CALIXTO GARCÍA

There is an almost incredible tale of Calixto García's survival in battle. During the Ten Years' War, he was out in the field with a small number of bodyguards when a force of about five hundred Spanish soldiers surprised him. With his men dying and the Spaniards about to capture him, García decided it was better to die than to allow himself, a general, to be taken prisoner. So he took out his revolver and shot himself under the chin.

Amazingly, the bullet came out between his eyes without entering the brain, and he recovered. For the rest of García's life he had a star-shaped scar on his forehead.

ers of the time, Luis Muñoz Rivera, had served in the short-lived autonomous government that gave Puerto Rico power over local affairs while remaining under Spanish rule. After the United States took over, he favored a similar arrangement: local self-government under U.S. rule.

The leadership in Cuba, however, favored independence and worried that the United States would stay in power and refuse to grant them independence. That fall, a commission that included Calixto García traveled to Washington to talk to Congress and President McKinley about Cuba's future. Even the temperamental old García realized the importance of friendly relations with the United States. "I have always been and am a very warm admirer of the United States," he said when he arrived in Washington. "I consider [American] intervention very beneficial to my country at the critical hours of the birth of our new republic."

García died of pneumonia that December, just two days after Spain and the United States signed the final peace treaty in Paris. It formalized that Spain had ceded Puerto Rico and the Philippines to the United States and had given up all claim of *sovereignty* over Cuba. It said nothing about whether the United States would keep or free its new possessions, but about Cuba (although not to the other places) it said that "any obligations assumed in this treaty by the United States with respect to Cuba are limited to the time of its occupancy thereof." To Cubans who had fought decades for independence, that clause in the treaty seemed to mean that the American occupation of Cuba would someday end, and that the island could then become sovereign.

But when would that day come? As 1898 turned into 1899, nobody knew. On January 1 of the New Year, the last remaining Spanish troops departed Cuba. It marked the end of the Spanish Empire in the Americas—and the arrival of the United States as a world power. "The Spanish-American War produced a revolutionary change in U.S. foreign policy," writes Hendrickson. "America went to war in 1898 with no plans for conquest or territorial expansion, but before the year was out the nation possessed an empire."

Defeating Yellow Fever

One of the first tasks taken on by General Leonard Wood, the new U.S.-appointed military governor of Cuba, was to get rid of yellow fever, a tropical disease that devastated local populations and accounted for many of the wartime casualties in 1898. No one knew how to prevent it, and no one knew how it was transmitted—except for a Cuban physician named Carlos Finlay. Finlay, who graduated from Jefferson Medical College in Philadelphia, figured out in the 1860s that the disease was transmitted by mosquitoes. Few paid attention until 1900, when he convinced Dr. Walter Reed, a U.S. Army surgeon in Cuba, to test his theory.

A yellow-fever hospital in Cuba in 1898.

Reed performed controversial experiments with people who willingly exposed themselves to the mosquito. Nearly all caught the fever. Finlay was proven to be right.

Then the task became prevention. Sanitation officials threw their best efforts into a campaign to eliminate stagnant water, where mosquitoes bred. It was not easy, at a time when most Cubans and Puerto Ricans had no running water and relied on storing it for washing and cooking. But the campaign succeeded, and yellow fever was almost entirely eliminated.

Cubans and Puerto Ricans welcomed the end of the disease. But the future political status of their islands remained in doubt.

A Commonwealth and a Republic

What to do with the territories it now occupied became the most pressing foreign policy issue for the United States as the nineteenth century ended. On the one hand, national memories of being a colony of Great Britain reminded Americans of the belief that people ought to rule themselves. On the other hand, some Americans were unsure about whether Cubans and Puerto Ricans were ready for self-government. Governor Wood, for instance, said to Secretary of State Elihu Root that giving Cubans independence would be difficult, because 60 percent were illiterate and there were "many sons and daughters of Africa." Historian Hugh Thomas said that Wood also wrote to President McKinley, saying, "I am giving the Cubans every chance to show what is in them, in order that they may either demonstrate their fitness or their unfitness for government."

There were similar feelings about Puerto Ricans. But in Puerto Rico the Americans felt less pressure to grant independence. The island was under direct U.S. military rule until 1900, when a civil government was established under American authority. Under the rules in those years, there was a governor and an executive council appointed by the U.S. president, a House of Representatives elected locally, and a nonvoting resident commissioner in the United States Congress.

Luis Muñoz Rivera became resident commissioner in 1910. In Washington he fought for more local autonomy, but without making Puerto Rico a state and without asking for outright independence. His great triumph was the 1917 passage of the Jones Act, which made Puerto Ricans U.S. citizens and established a legislature with more local authority. This let Puerto Ricans travel free of immigration restrictions between the states and the island. It also allowed those who lived in the states to vote in U.S. presidential elections—but those on the island could not vote, an arrangement that persists to this day.

Then, in 1952, Puerto Rico became a *commonwealth*, the status it has today. This means it is halfway between being an independent country and one of the fifty states, with a congressional representative who does not have a vote. In Puerto Rico today, most people are either in favor of statehood or of remaining a commonwealth. A smaller political party favors independence.

Cuba followed a different path. In Havana, still under U.S. military rule, Cuban leaders met to draft a new constitution for what they hoped would be a sovereign republic after the departure of the United States. The U.S. government decided it could not ignore the strong demands for

A ceremony in Old San Juan, Puerto Rico celebrates the establishment of the island as a commonwealth.

independence. But it was unwilling to let Cuba go completely on its own. The result was the Platt Amendment, which laid down conditions to which the Cuban government had to agree if it wanted independence. The most important was that the United States reserved the right to get involved in order to maintain "a government adequate for the protection of life, property, and individual liberty."

Some Cubans believed the Platt Amendment meant the republic about to be born was not really free, because it allowed the United States to send troops or to intervene in some other form whenever it disliked actions of the Cuban government. But it did not look as if the United States was going to back down. So by a margin of sixteen to eleven, with four absences, the Cuban Constitutional Convention accepted the Platt Amendment. In 1902 the Cuban republic was born, with Tomás Estrada Palma as its first president.

The Platt Amendment remained in effect until both countries agreed to eliminate it in 1934. For the next eighteen years Cuba was run by corrupt but fairly democratic governments, until Fulgencio Batista, a former elected president, took power as a dictator in 1952. He in turn was overthrown in 1959 by the communist revolution led by Fidel Castro.

The Spanish-American-Cuban War?

The conflict known as the Spanish-American War marked the end of one era and the beginning of another. Spain's defeat brought to an end the great empire that began with the arrival of Columbus in 1492, and that eventually gave birth to the Spanish-speaking nations of modern Latin America. It also began the rise of the United States as a force in international affairs, after utterly defeating in a few short weeks one of the traditional nations of old Europe.

But many Americans do not appreciate how important the war was for Cuban and Puerto Rican history. The war set both societies on the course they continue to follow today. Puerto Rico is still a commonwealth of the United

In modern-day Cuba, students fly Cuban flags during a parade held in Havana.

States. Cuba is a communist dictatorship, governed by people still angry at perceived injustices inflicted by the United States during the 1898 war and the four-year occupation that followed.

In his book *The War of 1898*, historian Louis A. Pérez argues that calling the conflict the Spanish-American war, without reference to Cubans, unfairly denies their participation. "Cubans seem to have disappeared, denied a role in the very outcome to which they had contributed so significantly," he wrote. Pérez also quotes former U.S. senator Dennis Chávez of New Mexico, a descendant of the Hispano people who were suspected of pro-Spanish, anti-American feelings during the war. In a speech while visiting Havana in 1948, for the fiftieth anniversary of the sinking of the *Maine*, Chávez said,

> I search in vain in the history books of my country for proper appreciation and recognition of the role which Cuban patriots played in the liberation of this country. It would seem that the Spanish-American War was fought only by American soldiers. . . . However, I wish to take this occasion to assure you that patriots throughout the world appreciate the valor and unselfishness of the valiant Cuban patriots who long before their American brothers arrived here, had fought and died for the liberation of their country.

Cubans certainly know that their ancestors fought to make their country independent. Their struggle is part of the history every child in Cuban schools has learned for more than a century.

Timeline

1868	The Puerto Rican pro-independence uprising known as the Grito de Lares begins.
	The Cuban pro-independence uprising known as the Grito de Yara begins; it leads to the Ten Years' War.
1868	The pact of Zanjón ends the Ten Years' War, and Cuba is still a Spanish colony.
1880–1895	Cubans and Puerto Rican exiles led by José Martí plot for independence.
1895	Grito de Baire begins the second Cuban War of Independence (1895–1898).
	José Martí and General Máximo Gómez fight for Cuban independence.
	Martí is killed in battle.
1896	Spanish Captain-General Valeriano Weyler orders the reconcentration policy in Cuba.
1897	U.S. president William McKinley is inaugurated.
	Spanish prime minister Antonio Cánovas del Castillo is assassinated; Práxides Mateo Sagasta becomes new prime minister.
	Sagasta fires General Weyler and replaces him with the moderate Captain General Ramón Blanco.
	Cuban General Antonio Maceo is killed in battle.
1898	Spain grants limited autonomy to Cuba and Puerto Rico.
	The U.S.S. *Maine* explodes in Havana Harbor.
	War is formally declared between Spain and the United States.
	U.S. ships bombard San Juan, Puerto Rico.
	The bombardment of Santiago begins.
	Santiago surrenders to U.S. troops; Cuban troops are not invited to enter the city.
	U.S. general Leonard Wood is named military governor of Santiago, beginning four years of U.S. military rule in Cuba.
	U.S. troops make their first landing in Puerto Rico.
	U.S. troops gain control of the city of Ponce, Puerto Rico.
	U.S. troops gain control of the city of Mayagüez, Puerto Rico.
	Spain and the United States sign a ceasefire agreement.

	General Calixto García and his Cuban forces are finally permitted to enter Santiago.
	Spanish troops complete their withdrawal from Puerto Rico.
	The Treaty of Peace in Paris is signed.
1899	The last of the remaining Spanish forces leave Cuba.
1900	A civilian government in Puerto Rico is instituted, under U.S. control.
1902	U.S. military rule of Cuba ends; the independent Republic of Cuba is proclaimed.

Glossary

anarchist A person who believes that all forms of governmental authority are unnecessary.

armistice A temporary agreement between warring nations to end the fighting.

autonomy A state of self-governance but not necessarily complete independence.

Caribbean Sea The body of water south of Florida that is the location of Cuba, Puerto Rico, and other islands.

cholera an acute, infectious disease characterized by profuse diarrhea, vomiting, cramps, etc.

commonwealth An organized political community.

conscripted Required to serve in a country's armed forces; drafted.

deported Forced to leave a country.

exile A person who was forced out of his or her native country.

guerrilla A member of an independent unit who uses harassing, aggressive ways in fighting.

Hispanos Spanish for "Hispanics"; in New Mexico, used as an English word to refer to the descendants of Spanish colonists.

insurgents People who are rebelling against an established government.

intervene To interfere in a conflict between nations or people.

legislature A group of people with the authority to make laws.

neutrality Refusal to take part in a war between two powers.

neutrality laws Regulations that prevent people from using U.S. soil to launch attacks against other countries.

reconcentration The process of bringing people or objects back into one place.

skirmish A small battle.

sovereignty Self-rule; national independence.

Further Information

Books

Engfer, Lee. *Cubans in America*. Minneapolis, MN: Lerner Books, 2005.

Zinn, Howard and Rebecca Stefoff. *A Young People's History of the United States: Columbus to the Spanish-American War*. New York: Seven Stories Press, 2007.

Web Sites

Library of Congress
www.loc.gov/rr/hispanic/1898
Hispanic resources, documents, and analysis from the Library of Congress.
PBS
www.pbs.org/crucible/
Website for the PBS documentary *Crucible of Empire: The Spanish-American War*.

New York Public Library
www.nypl.org/research/chss/epo/spanexhib/index.html
Hispanic resources from the New York Public Library.

Bibliography

Hendrickson, Kenneth E. *The Spanish-American War*. Westport, CT: Greenwood Press, 2003.

Montgomery, Charles. *The Spanish Redemption*. Berkeley and Los Angeles, CA: University of California Press, 2002.

O'Toole, G. J. A. *The Spanish War*. New York: W.W. Nortin & Co., 1986.

Pérez, Louis A. *The War of 1898: The United States and Cuba in History and Historiography*. Chapel Hill: University of North Carolina Press, 1998.

Thomas, Hugh. *Cuba: The Pursuit of Freedom*. New York: Da Capo Press, 1998.

Trask, David F. *The War with Spain in 1898*. New York: Macmillan Publishing, 1981.

Trebín Lastra, Frank. *Ybor City: The Making of a Landmark Town*. Tampa, FL: University of Tampa Press, 2006.

Index

Page numbers for illustrations are in boldface.

Antilles, the, 15
armistice, 59, 61
signing of, **4**, 5, 57, 63
Army of Liberation, Cuban, **29**, 29–30, 32, 50–52, 55, **61**
see also Spain, army of; United States, army of
autonomy, 28–29, 36, 62, 65, 66

Bagley, Worth, 40
balance of power, global, 5–6, 63, 69
Batista, Fulgencio, 68
Betances, Ramón, 14
Bolívar, Simón, 8, **8**

Cánovas del Castillo, Antonio, 34, 36
Castro, Fidel, 68
Cervera y Topete, Pascual, 54–55
Céspedes, Carlos Manuel de, 13, 16
Chávez, Dennis, 70
cigar factory workers, 15, 19
Cleveland, Grover, 34
clubs, independence, 16, 27
criollos, 8–9
Cuba, 6, **7**
heroes of, **26**
independence movement, 8–9, 11, 13–30, 36, 62–68
rebel government in, 39–40, 41, 42, 60
Spanish-American War in, 48–57, 69–71
U.S. occupation of, 57, 60–68, 70
Cuban Revolutionary Party, 19, 24
Cuban War of Independence, 21, 24, 25, 29–37

Daiquirí (Cuba), 49–51, **50**
Day, William, **4**
Dominican Republic, **7**, 15

Estrada Palma, Tomás, 24, **24**, 25, 28–29, 68

fairs, Cuban, 25–26, **26**
Finlay, Carlos, 64–65
flags, Cuban, **69**

García, Calixto, 49, 52, **58**, 59–60, 62–63
Gómez, Máximo, 20, **20**, 21, 30, 32
guerrilla warfare, 29, 33

Haya, Ignacio, 15
Hidalgo y Costilla, Miguel, 8
Hispanics/Hispanos, 11, 15–16, 43–48, **48**, 70
Hostos, Eugeinio María de, **12**, 14–15

Invasion of the West, 31–32
Irish immigrants, 9, 10

Jones Act, 66

Key West, Florida, independence activists in, 15, 16, 20, 27–28, 42

Lares uprising, 13, 14
Latin America, independence from Spain, 6, 8, 69
Linares Pomba, Arsenio, 50
López, Narciso, 11
Luna, Maximiliano, 47–48

Maceo, Antonio, 20, 30–32, 36
maps, **7**
Martí, José, **17**, 17–24, **22**, 25
Martínez Campos, Arsenio, 32
Martinez-Ybor, Vicente, 15
McKinley, William, **4**, 5, 34, **35**, 39
"Message to Garcia," 49
Mexican-American War, 6, 45
Mexico, independence from Spain, 8
Morales Lemus, José, 14, 15

Muñoz Rivera, Luis, 62, 66

New Mexico, Hispanos in, 45–48, 70
New York City, **43**
  independence activists in, 15, 17, 21, 26

O'Higgins, Bernardo, 8
Oñate, Juan de, 45
Otero, Miguel Antonio, 47

peace treaty. *See* armistice
Philippines, the, 6, 61, 63
Platt Amendment, 68
Puerto Rico, 6, **7**
  autonomy granted to, 36, 62, 65
  commonwealth status granted to, 66–67, **67**, 69–70
  independence movement, 8–9, 11, 13–15, 28, 67
  Spanish-American War in, 57, 69–70
  U.S. occupation of, 57, 61–62, 63

Quesada, Gonzalo de, 24–25, 39

reconcentration camps, 32–34, **33**, 36
Reed, Walter, 64–65
Revolutionary War, U.S., 8, 25, 28, 60
Roosevelt, Theodore, 52, 54
Rough Riders, 43, 47–48, **48**, 52

Sagasta, Práxedes Mateo, 36
San Juan Hill, Battle of, 48, 52–54, **53**
San Martin, José de, 8
Santiago (Cuba), **31**
  battle for, 52, 54–56, **55**, **56**, 59, 60
Shafter, William R., 49, 51, **56**
slavery, 8, 11, 65
South America, independence from Spain, 8
Spain
  army of, 30, **31**, 34, 50, 52, 54, 56, 57
  loss of empire, 5–6, 8–9, 11, 63, 68–69
  navy of, 54–56
  see also Hispanics/Hispanos

Spanish-American War
  battles of, 48–57
  declaration of, 5, **41**, 41–42
  end to, **4**, 5, 57, 59, 61, 63
  results of, 5–6, 57, 59–71

Tampa, Florida, **44**
  independence activists in, 15, 27, 42–44
Teller Amendment, 41, 60
Ten Years' War, 13–15, **14**, 25, 30, 62
veterans of, 19, 20, 22, 24
Toral, Jose, **56**

United States
  army of, 42–43, **43**, **44**, **50**, 50–52, **51**, 55
  becoming world power, 6, 63, 69
  independence activists in, 9–11, 13–17, 20–29
  intervention by, 34, 36–37, 39, 63
  navy of, 54–56
  occupation of Cuba by, 57, 60–68, 70
  in Spanish-American War, 21, **41**, 41–42, 48–57, 59
U.S.S. Maine, 36–37, **37**, **38**, 40

Varela, Félix, **9**, 9–11
voluntarios, 30, 36

Washington, George, 8
Weyler, Valeriano, 32–33, 34, 36
Wood, Leonard, 64, 65

Yara uprising, 13, 16, 25
Ybor City, Florida, independence activists in, 15, 43
yellow fever, elimination of, **64**, 64–65

About the Author

ROGER E. HERNÁNDEZ writes a nationally syndicated column distributed by King Features to some forty daily newspapers across the country. He is also writer in residence at the New Jersey Institute of Technology and author of *Cubans in America*. Hernández was born in Cuba and came to the United States as a child in 1965, when his parents fled the Castro regime.